Lefty Kreh's Solving Fly-Casting Problems

Lefty Kreh

Introduction by John Randolph

Foreword by Cathy & Barry Beck

Photo Assistance:

Chuck Edgehill

Larry Kreh

THE LYONS PRESS
Guilford, Connecticut
An imprint of The Globe Pequot Press

Printed in the United States of America

10 9 8 7 6 5 4 3 2 1

ISBN 978-1-59921-086-5

The Library of Congress has previously cataloged an earlier
(paperback) edition as follows:

Kreh, Lefty.
Solving fly-casting problems / Lefty Kreh; photo assistance, Chuck Edgehill.
p. cm.
ISBN 1-58574-034-9 (pbk.)
1. Fly casting. I. Title
SH454.2.K724 2000
799.1'24—dc21

00-42034

CONTENTS

INTRODUCTION

LEFTY THE WIZARD

I have known Bernard "Lefty" Kreh since 1978. During our first meeting, at West Yellowstone, Montana, he began trying to solve my lifelong casting problems. (He simultaneously began working on my photography.) During that trip we stopped in Yellowstone Park's Hayden Valley to photograph buffalo and moose. Two tourists standing nearby were having trouble with their point-and-shoot cameras. Lefty walked over, introduced himself, and spent twenty minutes giving them camera-use instructions until we dragged him away. That, you see, is Lefty Kreh—the ultimate teacher and friend to the world of klutzes, or as H. L. Mencken might have called them, the Klutzoizee.

We klutzes all need help with our casting, and Lefty long ago set himself on a lifelong mission: to teach us the right techniques—to teach every willing fly flinger, from Timbuktu to Petropavlosk, from East L.A. to Skowhegan. From the git-go Lefty understood one fundamental fact: You cannot fly fish effectively if you can't cast well.

Lefty has always found his highest values in wisdom derived from lore (knowledge acquired through experience). Lefty's wise messages are his stock-in-trade, and they are his gift to the world of fly fishing. A Lefty dictum posits that one cannot teach fly casting if he cannot emulate the mistakes that befuddle would-be fly casters. Yesterday on my office back lawn he once again demonstrated how to tail loops and how to cure them.

That is what this book is all about: How to analyze your casting problems and correct them. No one currently living, or even in the annals of our sport's rich history, has done more to correct casting problems than

Lefty Kreh. When he teaches—and he teaches during all his waking hours—this is how he turns klutzes into fine casters. (I am a good caster now; thank you Lefty.)

If you take this book and use it interactively with your lawn practice, you will quickly become a better fly caster. You should practice following Lefty's recommended techniques, and you should practice every day to become an expert caster by the end of a summer. As Lefty has noted, you cannot become a successful fly fisher unless you become a good caster. That does not imply that you must cast 100 feet of fly line efficiently and accurately. It does mean that you must be able to cast a straight line accurately without tailing loops, line waves, or unwanted casting hooks to a distance of at least 40 feet. That will get you into the magic ballpark where you can catch fish.

More importantly, it will get you to a plateau from which you can see the other, higher, attainable, plateaus, those levels of casting that separate the expert fly fisher from the beginners and intermediates. Then, after your tailing loops have been cured, and your unwanted casting hooks are straightened, and your backslaps are history, and you don't "snap the whip" any me, well, then you can start learning the "fishing casts," messing up the casts where necessary to achieve more "natural presentations."

You'll soon discover, if you head to a coast, that casting on saltwater is a whole new ballgame, with its own technique requirements, including "combat casting" in 20- to 30-mile-per-hour winds. By then you will probably have come to appreciate all the Kreh books on the subject of casting. In fact you will have learned that casting is truly the Yellow Brick Road to fly-fishing success. Do I dare say that Lefty Kreh is the Wizard? You bet. He's also a good friend.

—JOHN RANDOLPH
JULY 2000

FOREWORD

I remember my first casting lesson with Lefty. It was a couple years after Barry and I were married. My trout fishing was coming along pretty well when we decided to try saltwater fly fishing. After my first humiliating trip to the Florida Keys, I was ready to give up fly fishing altogether. Barry called Lefty in a panic and asked if he could help me learn to cast the bigger salt-water rods and heavier lines.

My stomach was all butterflies during our trip down to Lefty's house and by the time we arrived I was a nervous wreck. Lefty took me to a little pond close to his house that he uses for lessons and promptly told me, "Now, if you want sympathy, go see your mother." I was literally shaking in my shoes. Later I would learn that this was one of his favorite lines and he uses it to break the ice. He then put his hand on top of mine on the rod handle and proceeded to teach me.

Over time that afternoon, I learned, in the first of many casting lessons that I would take from Lefty over the years. To this day, whenever I fish with him, I still take advantage of every minute I can to learn something from him.

Barry first met Lefty as a teenager on an evening at the fabled Letort Spring Run. He tells the story all the time whenever Lefty's name comes up, and it's a good example of Lefty's personality and skill. A group of locals sat together on Fox's Meadow — Vince Marinaro, Charlie Fox, Ross Trimmer, and Jim Bashline. Barry was the new kid, on the outskirts. Jim Bashline had been watching a nice Letort brown that was feeding in a very narrow channel tight against the far bank. In front of the fish were two huge weed beds. Jim kept talking about how he'd like to see the fish caught but there didn't seem to be a way to get a decent presentation to the fish. The group then heard a car door in the background and another angler joined them. Soon Barry was shaking hands with Lefty Kreh.

The fish talk continued while Bashline's trout kept feeding. Finally somebody said, "Lefty, why don't you try that fish?" and Barry thought, "Wow, talk about being put on the spot."

Lefty smiled and said, "Sure. Why not?"

He slowly moved upstream into a casting position while the rest of the group watched. After three quick false casts, Lefty's razor-sharp loop sailed toward the rising fish. There was no room for error: the fly had to land within a foot of the feeding fish, and, of course, it did. One cast, one quiet sip: one Letort brown.

What impressed Barry most was not the cast and not the fish, but the angler's reaction. Lefty was as excited as if it was his first trout. After releasing the fish and receiving serious praise from the group (and what a group!) he smiled and said, "Boy, I got lucky." But there was no ego there, no showing off; just a skilled angler doing what he does best and really enjoying it. That's Lefty.

That's the kind of attitude that backs up this book—work hard to get good because there's a lot to enjoy in this sport. Lefty's wisdom seems boundless, but each little lesson in this book teaches you something specific and essential. The greater your range of technical skills, the greater your chances that you, too, might one day make a single, amazing cast in front of your friends and catch a fine fish in a tricky spot. When you let that fish go, think of Lefty.

Good fishing,
Cathy & Barry Beck
May 2007

1 LEFTY'S PRINCIPLES OF FLY CASTING

Please study this section before attempting the casts in this book. These principles will improve your casting in general and enable you to duplicate the more specialized casts.

1. If you are right-handed, the right foot should be positioned to the rear and the left foot slightly forward. Left-handers should do the reverse.
2. When the rod stops at the end of the backcast, and again at the end of the forward cast, the thumb should be positioned behind the rod handle in a plane that points toward the target. This transmits energy better away from, and back to, the target, and improves accuracy. For example, twisting the thumb to the right diverts energy from the target.
3. The elbow should not be elevated during the cast. If you walk up to a shelf and place your elbow on it without lifting it—that is the correct elevation of the elbow. During the entire cast the elbow should remain in contact with the imaginary shelf, and the angle of the backcast is determined by the rod hand. By keeping the elbow on the imaginary shelf, it permits you to move the rod further back; on the forward cast, it helps eliminate tailing loops.
4. The rod is a flexible lever. The longer you move it through the back- and forward casts, the more it helps you with the cast.
5. All of the line should be lifted from the water *before* making the first backcast. You can't make a backcast until you get the end of the line moving.
6. All casts are divided into two parts. First, there is a relatively long stroke. Second, there is a very brief speed-up-and-stop at the end of the long stroke. The line and fly will travel in the direction that the rod tip speeds up and stops at the end of the cast. The tip should almost always stop in an upward direction on the backcast and usually parallel to the water on the forward cast.

7. The loop size and casting distance are determined by the distance the rod tip travels during the speed-up-and-stop in the final moment of the cast. The shorter the distance the tip moves during the speed-up-and-stop, the smaller the loop. The faster the rod tip moves over that short distance, and the quicker the tip stops, the greater the line speed and the longer the cast.
8. For short casts, the rod can be raised vertically on the backcast. But to make longer casts, the rod needs to travel well behind the angler. During the cast, including the speed-up-and-stop, the rod tip and hand need to travel at an upward angle and end in a straight line away from the target. However, the elbow must remain level. This calls for a side cast. To accomplish this cast, use only the forearm (just like hitchhiking). Using the full arm will ruin the cast. Make sure that the elbow stays at the same height throughout both back- and forward cast and that the hand and rod tip travel at an upward angle on the backcast. Until the rod has passed behind the caster on the backcast, the tip should stay below the head.

2 FOOTWORK IS IMPORTANT

The position of your feet is often ignored, but it is critical to good fly casting. For a very short cast, you only need to move the arm. For longer casts, the body should move fluidly. You can throw a dart by moving the arm, but if you throw a spear, the body moves through much more motion. So it is with casting long distances.

With the right-hander, positioning the right foot forward makes it very difficult to move backward on the cast.

Some anglers stand so that both feet are almost parallel. But this doesn't permit them to move the upper body back or forward, which constricts the cast.

If you are right-handed, the right foot should be behind the body. If you are left-handed, the left foot should be to the rear. This allows the body to move to the rear and well forward, as shown here.

3 INEFFICIENT ROLL CAST

The roll cast is the one cast that almost all fly fishermen do poorly. Yet next to the basic cast, the roll cast is the most important. These two photos demonstrate why most people have problems with it.

In a poorly executed roll cast, the rod hand is held high, often above the shoulder with the rod pointing in a near-vertical position. The fly line drapes slightly behind the angler.

The rod sweeps forward and down toward the surface in front of the fisherman.

Let's examine why this is not a good idea. The size of your loop is determined by the length of the speed-up-and-stop at the end of a cast. The line will go in the direction that the rod tip speeds up and stops.

By holding the hand high and sweeping the rod tip down and forward, you force the rod to throw the forward cast around the widest circle possible. What line energy is not directed around the circle is thrown on the water in front of the angler, creating a tangled mess.

EFFICIENT ROLL CAST

When we make a roll cast, it is usually because we cannot make a good backcast. So, we have to modify the backcast. But we should never modify the forward cast. *We should make what would be a normal forward cast.* To efficiently make a roll cast, do the following:

Position the rod tip as far behind you as the fishing condition will allow. Your elbow should be held at its normal level, and your rod hand should be well below your shoulder, as shown in the photo. Allow the line to stop so that the surface tension can grip the line and give the rod something to pull against.

During the forward cast, the rod hand should move straight ahead. If your hand rises, you will throw a bigger loop. Make a normal forward cast as though the water is at eye level. If the rod tip stops while diving toward the surface, you will get the usual pileup of the line at the end of the cast. If your rod hand travels straight ahead in a sideways arc, your fly line will travel straight ahead as it comes up off the water. If you make the cast correctly, the loop will resemble what is shown in this photo.

ELEVATED ROLL CAST

There are many times when an elevated roll cast can help. For this cast, the line is directed upward on the forward roll. This causes the fly and much of the leader to lift vertically from the water surface. Let me cite several occasions when this is desirable. When using a popping bug, a conventional backcast often causes the bug to dive before it exits the water, which makes a fish-disturbing sound. By using an elevated roll cast, the fly line lifts the bug almost vertically from the surface. This technique can also be used to lift a dry fly from the surface. When you have slack line lying in front of you, an elevated roll cast can lift the line from the water, making an easy backcast possible. Another useful purpose of this cast is to rid a fly of grass caught on the hook. Make a slow, deliberate, elevated roll cast, and when all the line is out of the water (but the fly is still under water), make a powerful backcast. Water clings to the grass, and the hook acts like a shear. In most cases, the grass is severed from the hook. After the backcast, the fly can be delivered to the target.

It is easier to make the elevated roll cast if the rod tip is positioned low behind you. Instead of your rod hand traveling parallel to the surface, as with a conventional forward roll cast, your hand travels upward at about a 45-degree angle (see arrow direction). Be sure the rod tip stops in that direction. Note that the leader is rising straight up from the water.

6 LONG-DISTANCE ROLL CAST

There are many occasions when you need to make a cast beyond 50 feet, but you have only 20 feet behind you for the backcast. This is especially true when there are trees or when there is a bank behind you.

You need to have considerable line out—at least 40 feet or more is helpful. Make a weak backcast. The purpose of the weak backcast is to lift the line out of the water and let much of it pass behind you. The key is this: The line end (where the leader is attached) should fall back to the water about a rod length in front of you. The arrow in the photograph indicates the perfect spot where the line end falls; if it falls much farther in front of or too far behind this point, it is difficult to make the long roll cast. Note that the line loop behind the angler is in the air. If you allow the line behind you to fall to the surface, the cast is very difficult to make.

The forward roll cast should begin the moment the fly line end touches the water and the line loop behind you is in the air. A single haul really helps on the forward roll.

7 SIDE ROLL CAST

The side roll cast allows you to roll a fly underneath overhanging structure and to fish where most people can't get a fly. While it appears to be a difficult cast, it is not—that is, as long as you follow a few simple rules.

Bring the rod back until it is vertical and tilted slightly behind you. Allow the line to stop on the surface (it only needs to pause a heartbeat) so that you can properly load the rod for the forward cast.

Lay the rod over, as shown by the arrow. Be sure not to drop the rod tip; keep the rod level.

Here is the important part of the cast. Note how the rod at the beginning of the forward side roll cast is parallel to the surface. The line and fly will travel in the direction that the rod tip speeds up and stops at the end of the cast. *It is essential with a side roll cast that the rod tip travel parallel to the water during the speed-up-and-stop.* If you want the loop to travel parallel to the surface and 2 feet above the water, then the speed-up-and-stop must travel the same path.

If the rod tip traveled as described, the line will unroll and lay out perfectly.

Note that the rod should not travel at a downward angle during the speed-up-and-stop, as shown here.

If the tip travels downward during the speed-up-and-stop, the line will loop up and crash.

8 AERIAL ROLL CAST

The aerial roll cast is very useful when there is little room behind or overhead and you need to make a short cast. The arrow points to the limb just above the angler's head. This is exactly the kind of obstacle this cast is designed to over come. But this cast is effective only to about 15 feet.

Extend enough line and leader outside the rod tip to reach the target. Grasp the fly by the bend of the hook, so that it won't impale you when you release it. Point the rod at the target with the rod close to the surface.

Swiftly sweep the rod upward, but stop it before the tip reaches the vertical position. This will cause the line to unroll in the air behind you, as shown in the photo. Don't let go of the fly.

Hold the fly just tight enough to make the roll cast. As soon as the rod tip stops its upward motion, sweep it down and toward the target.

If you have clenched the fly correctly, the forward cast will pull the fly from your fingers, and the line will travel to the target.

LEARN TO TIGHTEN YOUR LOOP

For years anglers have been told that large or open fly line loops didn't travel far because of air resistance. The real reason is that when you form a large loop, you throw the energy of the cast around a curve. A small loop causes most of the energy to be directed away from or toward the target. Almost all fly casters throw loops too large. Here is an exercise that will tighten your loops. But it must be an exercise—if you start casting, you'll ruin the exercise and open your loops.

Before beginning to cast, stand sideways, so that you can both look at your rod tip and watch your line during the entire cast.

With the line in front of you, play a mental game. As you begin the backcast, look at the rod tip and try to backcast so that the line will strike or slam against the tip. If you halt the speed-up-and-stop too early in the stroke, the line will indeed hit the rod tip. But if you make the speed-up-and-stop correctly, you will get a tight loop that resembles the one in the photo.

As you make the forward cast, continue to look at the rod tip as you throw the line at it, and you will form a loop like this. False cast as much as you can during the exercise, and don't drop the forward cast to the ground or water after each complete cast.

If you don't look at the rod tip and do not try make the line crash against the tip, you get a loop like the one in these photos. By trying to hit the rod tip with the line, the direction of flight forms a tight loop. What most people do is duck the rod tip away from the fly line in back and front, forming wide loops, as shown here.

10 WHEN THE WIND IS ON YOUR WRONG SIDE

If you are right-handed and the wind is blowing from the right, the wind can cause the line and fly to blow against you on the forward cast. It's no fun to be stuck by a sharp hook. Fortunately, there is an easy way to accomplish a good cast with never a fear of being hit by the line or fly. Best of all, you can use fluid, normal casting strokes.

When the wind is blowing from the right, many right-handers will cast as shown here. This restricts both body and arm movements and makes longer casts difficult.

Instead, make the backcast to the side as shown here. This keeps the line well away from the body.

On the forward cast, you need only tilt or lean the rod tip to the left slightly. There is no need to tilt it a lot. Because the wind is blowing from the right and the rod is tilted, the line will flow to the left of the caster. The best feature about using this cast is that your body and arm can flow naturally, which results in a longer cast.

IN
LACES

There are many occasions, especially while trout fishing, when your rod is too long to allow you to cast in close quarters. This occurs frequently on small streams. Here is a simple trick that will often allow you to make a cast in this situation. Admittedly, you can't make a long cast this way—but in such tight quarters, a short cast is usually called for.

Slide your hand up until it touches the stripping guide (arrow). Now make a regular cast. You have shortened the rod dramatically. It helps to use the double haul, but it isn't necessary.

12 CHANGE-IN-DIRECTION CAST

This is a cast you can use for a number of situations. It permits you to quickly move the fly from one spot to another with only one backcast. It is best for casts shorter than 40 feet. Here are some examples of when the cast can be useful:

1. Your fly is on the water when a trout rises off to one side. Using this cast, you can deliver a fly to the rising trout within seconds with only one backcast.
2. You are stripping a fly to a fish when suddenly a better fish appears off to the right or left. This frequently happens when fishing saltwater flats. Within seconds, this cast will let you throw the fly to the second fish.
3. You have made a cast up and across the stream, the fly has drifted downstream, and you now want to place the fly upstream again. No need for several false casts—just use the change-in-direction cast with one backcast.

The key to making this cast is placing the backcast in the opposite direction of the target.

In this photo, the angler has been casting to his left when a fish rises in the direction he is now facing. Keeping the rod low, the line is dragged along the surface as shown until the rod is pointing at the target. This allows him to make a backcast directly away from the target. If the rod is elevated during this part of the cast, it will be difficult to make a good backcast.

The arrow points in the direction of the target. When pointing the rod tip toward the target and immediately before the backcast, do not stop—keep the line moving. When the rod is low and pointing at the target, make a backcast directed straight away from the target. A haul on the backcast often improves it.

If the line is directed away from the target on the backcast, a normal forward cast is easy. The time it takes to make the change of direction is probably no more than 3 or 4 seconds.

13 THE TUCK CAST

Many trout fishermen would rather catch their quarry on the surface, but most of the time trout feed and rest near the bottom. A common problem anglers encounter is that during the drift, the current pulls on the line and prevents the fly from getting to the bottom. The tuck cast gets the fly deep in the water column before the downstream drift begins.

The object of a tuck cast is to make the leader and fly tuck under the fly line as it falls to the water. Because considerable slack occurs, the weighted fly can sink unimpeded toward the bottom before the line and current begin to pull on it. The result is that the fly gets closer to the bottom before the drift.

You have to do several things to make a good tuck cast. First, you need to make the forward cast very high—well above your head. Unless the cast is made high, the leader and fly will not have enough room to tuck under. Too many people direct the line downward on the forward cast. Second, you must overpower the forward cast. Hauling on the forward cast generates more line speed. Third, the rod must stop dead at the end of the cast. If the cast is high, traveling very fast, and the rod stops dead, the speeding line pulls the rod tip forward. When the tip recoils, it causes the fly and leader to tuck under the line. The longer the leader, within reason, the greater the tuck. Obviously, the faster the line travels, the deeper the rod is flexed, and the greater the tuck.

Some people recommend pulling back after the rod stops, but this actually removes some of the tuck from the cast. By tilting the rod to the left or right, you can make a tuck cast that results in both the fly tucking and curving to the left or right.

Note in the photo how high the rod has stopped. The circle indicates where the fly has tucked well back under the fly line.

14 STACK CAST

One of the first things you learn about fishing dry flies is that you need a drag-free drift. The leader and line must have a series of shallow waves or slack so that the fly can drift naturally with the current, as opposed to dragging along the surface. The most common way to obtain slack in the leader is to overpower the forward cast, which at the end of the cast causes shock to develop in the leader and line. The problem with overpowering the cast is that you are not sure where the shock waves will drop your fly. Accuracy suffers as a result.

There is a much better way to present the line and fly and to guarantee many small, desirable waves in the line and leader. This cast has many names. The one I prefer is *stack cast,* because you throw the line in such a manner that the front end stacks the leader and line in waves on the surface. Another advantage of the stack cast is that it is easily made at any distance the caster can throw. Once mastered, you can make better drag-free drifts and hook more trout.

For best results, it is essential that you make a low backcast, as shown here.

The low backcast permits the angler to make a climbing forward cast, as shown here. It is very important that this forward cast isn't overpowered: If too much line speed develops, the line will recoil and spoil the cast. It is essential to make the climbing forward cast a very "soft" one.

As soon as the speed-up-and-stop occurs, the direction of the cast has been determined. As soon as the rod stops, drop the tip toward the surface, and waves will occur (as shown here). Failure to drop the rod immediately after the stop will remove much of the slack, as you will see in the next section.

15 DROPPING THE ROD FOR SLACK

Many trout fishermen have trouble developing slack in the leader and line as a dry fly falls to the water. Fortunately, the solution is pretty simple. First, you need to understand why slack is not there.

If you make a shock cast or a stack cast, or any other cast to develop those desirable waves in your dry-fly leader, they will never happen if your rod remains in the position shown in this photo. The line falls to the surface and removes slack if the rod remains upright, because the sag in the line "droops" back toward the angler.

The moment the rod tip stops on the forward cast, drop the entire rod parallel to the surface, as shown here. Notice the resultant slack in the line.

16 RIPPING LINE OFF THE WATER

Many fish are never caught because of improper backcasts. Any fish in shallow, calm water is easily frightened, or at least alerted to danger. This is especially true with trout in quiet water or bonefish, tarpon, and permit on a saltwater flat.

A floating fly line is held on the water by surface tension. If the angler simply sweeps the rod up during a backcast, it causes the line to be ripped from the surface, which makes a considerable disturbance (see the splash—relatively straight line of torn water—indicated by the arrow).

Note the disturbance made by ripping the line from the surface. *Never make a cast until all the line is free of the water.* The leader and fly can be under water. When you first try this, you may be lifting the rod too slowly. If so, the line just outside of the rod tip will droop, and you will have difficulty getting the line free of the water. You must lift the rod fast enough that you don't have a sag and not so fast that you rip the line free.

There are other problems you avoid by getting the line free before making the backcast. If you make a backcast while some of the line is on the water, the rod bends with the effort. When the line springs free, it causes the rod to jolt. This places shock waves in the line that can harm the cast or puts knots in your leader. Another problem you avoid is being overwhelmed by long lines. Most casters have difficulty picking up a long line. When you make sure you have all the line free of the surface before making the backcast, you'll be surprised how much better you can pick up a long line.

17 THROWING AN EXTRA-HIGH BACKCAST

There are many fishing locations where an extra-high backcast is required: mangrove creeks; trout streams with overhanging brush or trees; and along the coast, where there are high shorelines behind the caster. In short, an extra-high backcast is desired by almost all fly fishermen.

(Facing page): In a conventional backcast stroke, the rod is tipped downward behind the angler as a high backcast is attempted. But your hand can only go as far as shown in the photo. This often results in a backcast that is not nearly high enough.

Position your thumb underneath the rod and allow the rod tip to just touch the water before you begin the backcast (arrow). Remember, the angle of the backcast is determined by the direction in which the rod tip speeds up and stops. If you don't place the rod tip at the surface before beginning the backcast, you reduce your ability to throw a very high backcast.

With the thumb underneath the rod at the start of the cast and the rod tip at the surface, you can make a near-vertical backcast. As soon as the backcast is made, turn the hand around and make a normal forward cast.

18 MENDING LINE PROPERLY

Most fly fishermen know that once a portion of the line drifts downstream of the leader and fly, the belly in the line will pull out the desired slack from the leader. This causes the fly to drag unnaturally, reducing your chances of catching fish. To avoid this, an angler will often mend the line (lay a curve upstream in the line) during the drift. *This usually results in removing most of the slack in the leader, because the slack line used to create the mend is pulled from the leader end.* The following four photos demonstrate how to get a drag-free drift and still have plenty of slack in your leader.

The angler has made a cast and correctly produced slack in the foward leader and line.

The angler realizes that he has to place the line upstream of the fly, or his fly will drag. A mend is actually slack line in a curve that is created by rolling the rod over. But, by holding onto the line in his hand, the slack required to make the mend is pulled from the leader and the front of the line. Note how straight the line and leader are.

To maintain the slack in the front of the line and in the leader, carefully wiggle the rod tip to feed loose line through the rod to get the desired amount of slack needed for the mend. Be careful not to wiggle the tip so violently that you pull slack from the front of the line.

Now, if you make a gentle upstream mend, you will not disturb the waves in the front of the line and leader, as shown here.

19 REACH CAST

Many fly fishermen understand that once the belly of the line is downstream of the fly, it will cause the fly to be dragged unnaturally. This can be fatal for the dry-fly fisherman. A downstream belly will also affect a streamer retrieve. As long as the line remains upcurrent of the fly, it has little or no effect on the fly. The reach cast positions all of the line upcurrent during the drift.

A reach cast can be made at any distance the angler can throw the line. You need only perform a few simple functions to make a good reach cast.

The forward cast must travel slowly and be directed well above the angler's head. You need a high, slow-traveling flight, so that you will have ample time to perform the cast.

The moment the rod stops on the forward cast, lay the rod over, as the photo shows. The farther you can reach upcurrent, the more line will be placed there.

Where anglers often fail with the reach cast is in not realizing that they are placing a lot of slack line upstream. If they grip the line while laying the rod tip over, the slack will be pulled from the front end of the line—spoiling any possibility of a drag-free drift. *What is vital to a good reach cast is that during the time the rod is being placed upcurrent, you must allow slack to slide through your left hand.* And, if the forward cast is directed upward (similar to a stack cast) you can put additional waves in your leader, which ensures a longer drag-free drift.

If the forward cast is high and slow, if the rod is laid to the side properly, and if the slack line is allowed to flow through your left hand, the line will lay down on the water like this.

20 CONTROLLING LINE ON THE SHOOT

Most casters release the line when they shoot to the target. There are reasons for not doing this. The only time I suggest releasing the line on the shoot is when you just want to obtain greater distance and are not attempting to hit a target.

If you cast a plug with a spinning reel, you often cast the lure farther than the target, and then stop the lure's flight at any point with your thumb or finger. Yet fly fishermen let go of the line on the shoot and hope that by some chance it will land on the target. Fly line often does not flow smoothly through the stripping guide. By controlling the line with an O-ring formed by the first finger and thumb, line can become untangled before it goes through the guides, and you can stop the fly's flight when you wish.

Many people have trouble seeing quarry, especially bonefish. When they finally see the quarry, they make a cast, release the line on the shoot, and take their eyes off the fish to locate the line. When they recover the line and look up, they never find the fish. If you're shooting line correctly, you can keep your eye on the target.

If you release the line on the shoot, you surrender any control of the line, and tangles can get caught in the stripping guide.

With the line flowing through the O-ring formed by the first finger and thumb, the angler has the line under control and can stop the fly over the target. It's also possible to keep the fish in sight throughout the cast. You can begin a retrieve as soon as the fly touches the water.

21 EXTRA-EFFORT CAST

A poor backcast occurs when a fly caster has to pick up more fly line than he or she can easily handle. The long line is lifted from the water by raising the rod vertically. Because the angler is straining, this often results in a deep sag in the line before the backcast is made. Because a forward cast cannot be made until all the sag has been removed, a poor forward cast results.

Bringing the rod up vertically for a backcast almost always forces the rod tip to dive back and down at the end of the stroke (top arrow), which results in a deep sag (bottom arrow).

To eliminate the sag, touch the rod tip to the water before starting the backcast. Make sure all slack is removed between the rod tip and the fly (arrow at right). Make a side backcast so that the rod tip travels as if up a wedge (long arrow). Be sure that the rod tip remains below your head until it passes behind your body. If the rod tip is above your head before that point, it will dip on the stroke and cause a sag in the line. Once the rod tip is beyond your body and is still climbing that wedge, make a speed-up-and-stop. Be sure the tip stops in an upward direction. The loop behind you will be tight and straight. You can then come forward with an effective side or vertical cast.

22 USING A MOUSETRAP

A mousetrap can improve your accuracy while you are having fun. Cock a trap and set it on the ground approximately 25 feet away. Later, you can extend this distance. You must use a weighted fly or popping bug for this accuracy game. Clip the point and bend from the hook so that the fly doesn't tangle in the grass.

Start trying to hit the trap. Almost every fly caster will find that they don't hit the trap often, no matter how good they are. During the first dozen casts, you will find that you overshoot, undershoot, or throw to the right and perhaps to the left. In other words, you don't know where the fly is going. But, as you concentrate, you will begin to see fewer wild casts. Soon you will be throwing the fly consistently closer to the trap.

If you are one of those fly fishermen who makes your forward cast with the rod tip leaning slightly out from the body, you will soon discover a casting flaw. Nearly every cast will hook to the side. If you are right-handed, you will see that whenever you have been casting a weighted fly, you have been throwing a left hook at the end of the cast. Here's why: The line and fly will go in the direction that the rod tip speeds up and stops. If the rod is tilted out and you stop quickly, a right-hander's rod tip curves to the left, forming that left hook in the cast.

The trap will soon make you see that for a really accurate cast, the rod tip must come forward in a true vertical plane during the speed-up-and-stop.

23 USING A HULA HOOP

The Hula Hoop will improve almost anyone's loop control. Many people can throw a loop so narrow it might go through a doorway. But the Hula Hoop exercise soon demonstrates that although you may throw a tight loop, you may be very inaccurate with it.

Tape a Hula Hoop to a post. Stand about 30 feet away and try throwing your loop through the hoop. Don't be ashamed if you're not doing well at first. Because you are concentrating on loop control, after a number of misses, you'll find you can occasionally get one through the hoop. Keep the exercise up. When you can throw eight out of ten casts through the loop, increase the distance. After much practice, you'll be able to throw the loop through the hoop regularly at 50 feet.

24 SKIP CAST

There are many occasions in salt and fresh water when the ability to skip a fly under a boat dock or overhanging trees will help you catch more fish. This is called a skip cast.

This is one of many casts you will have difficulty making if you bring the rod up vertically on the backcast, because the forward cast, seen here, is moving upward.

To make a good skip cast, you have to set up the forward cast with a very low backcast. It is ideal to bring the line back almost parallel to the surface, so turn your hand to move the rod across the surface (arrow).

Do you remember how to skip a stone on the water? You must do two things: Throw it fast enough for the stone skip, and don't aim the stone where the skipping will end. Instead, you strike the water fairly close in front of you.

You do the same thing with the fly line. However, the line only skips once as it travels to the target. The double haul really helps in a skip cast, because it develops the required extra line speed. After the low side cast is made, carry the rod forward nearly parallel to the water, with the rod tip only a foot or so above the surface. Aim the cast so that the fly line bounces off the water just in front of you. The arrow in the photo shows where the line hit the surface just in front of my body. The line is now traveling parallel to the surface so that it will skim back under the overhanging branches.

25 TAILING LOOPS

Just about every fairly good fly caster will make tailing loops from time to time. I believe there is more misinformation concerning what causes tailing loops than in any other facet of fly casting.

A tailing loop happens when the upper portion of the loop is directed on the same plane as the bottom of the loop. A tailing loop will not occur if the upper portion of the loop remains above the bottom throughout the forward cast.

All tailing loops are caused when the rod tip is directed straight ahead during the speed-up-and-stop. Remember that the line will always follow the direction of the rod tip at the end of the speed-up-and-stop.

Some people claim that a tailing loop occurs if you shock or jar a rod to a stop. This is not true. A tailing loop only occurs if the rod is shocked while going straight ahead at the speed-up-and-stop. Demonstrate this to yourself by making a jarring shock while going straight ahead at the speed-up-and-stop: A tailing loop occurs. Then, try making a jarring stop with the tip, but stop in a slightly downward direction: No tailing loop occurs. Others claim that a tailing loop occurs if you start the forward cast too soon. That's because people who stop too soon on the forward cast tend to drive the tip straight ahead as they stop.

There are a number of ways to eliminate a tailing loop. If you have brought the rod forward and the top of the loop remains above the bottom, and if you stop with a slight dipping of the rod tip, you'll be able to keep the loop in the desired position and no tailing will occur.

Here is a typical tailing loop. Most tailing loops are caused by casters raising the rod hand above the shoulder on the backcast. On the forward cast, the hand travels in a downward plane. The rod tip stops going straight ahead, driving the upper loop down and into the bottom of the loop.

If the thumb stops going straight ahead, as shown in the circle, a tailing loop results, because the tip has been forced to stop going straight ahead. This drives the line into itself.

This is the easiest way to a eliminate tailing loop. The backcast has been made and the elbow is not elevated during the back- or the forward cast (see "Lefty's Principles of Fly Casting," page 1). *No matter where the forward cast begins, the rod hand must travel at that height throughout the forward cast. If the hand drops even a few inches, you will probably get a tailing loop.*

If the rod hand comes forward parallel to the water and the speed-up-and-stop finishes with the thumb pointing straight ahead, as shown in the circle, the top of the loop remains on the top. No tailing loop occurs.

26 LOOSE LINE AT YOUR FEET

If you have just replaced your fly and there is line lying on the water in front of you, there is a quick way of getting the line to the target. Remember, you can make a cast after you have the line end moving.

Lower the rod tip close to the water and sweep it smoothly to the left. It is important to keep the rod tip close to the water as you sweep the rod. This allows you to make a better backcast.

Now sweep the rod to your right, being sure to keep the rod tip close to the surface.

Watch the end of the fly line, where the leader is attached. Once it begins to move, you can begin the backcast. For maximum efficiency, you want the backcast to be directed opposite the target. To do this, begin the backcast when the rod is pointed *toward* the target. Remember, the end of the fly line must be moving at this point.

Make the backcast directly away from the target. The closer the rod tip is to the water, the easier it is to make the backcast. A single haul on the backcast will also help to get the line moving.

27 CATCHING THE LINE TO EXAMINE OR REPLACE THE FLY

There are times when you want to replace a fly, or check the fly or leader. There is no need to strip in most of the line. I have used this trick for more than forty years and have never hooked my hand. *Just make the cast gentle.*

With no more than 20 feet of line in front of you, lower the rod to the surface and make a gentle backcast, being sure to tilt the rod slightly to the right. This will cause the line to slowly move backward and to your side. If you made the backcast too hard, the fly line will be too fast for you to catch it. Just make another backcast if it seems too fast. It takes just a few practice casts for you to judge how gentle the backcast should be.

Spread your thumb as far as you can from your fingers. As the line slowly sails past you, trap it loosely between the thumb and the hand. You want the line to be able to slide between the thumb and fingers, so don't grasp the line tightly.

The moment your hand catches the line, the rest of the line will be flowing behind you, as shown in the photo. Sweep the rod forward gently. Don't allow the line to strike the surface behind you.

Allow the line to slowly sweep forward through your hand until you feel the leader. At that moment, clench the leader tightly. You are now able to repair the leader or check or replace the fly.

28 ROD ANGLE

Some years ago a national magazine editor asked ten of the top fly casting instructors what they felt were the major mistakes made by fly casters. Eight said that the most serious problem was the habit of starting the backcast with the rod held too high. Remember: No cast can be made until you move the end of the fly line.

If you begin your backcast with the rod this high (or higher) you are almost surely going to put a sag in your backcast.

The rod will probably move beyond a vertical position before you get the line end moving. Since the line will go in the direction that the rod tip speeds up and stops, the line will be thrown *back and down,* as shown in the photo. The arrow indicates the direction of the speed-up-and-stop.

Because the line has been directed back and downward, on longer casts the line frequently strikes the water, as shown here.

You can't make a forward cast until you get the line end moving. But when you begin the backcast too high, most of the forward cast is utilized in removing the deep sag from the line. This usually results in the rod tip traveling forward and down on the front cast and creates the large, undesirable loop, as shown here.

If your rod tip is near the surface (especially on a longer cast) as shown by the arrow, and all slack has been removed, you can quickly move the line end.

If a low backcast is desired, the rod can travel upward on a low slant (long arrow) and result in a tight loop at the angle you stop the rod tip (small arrow), with no sag.

If a more elevated backcast is desired, the rod travels upward and stops at that angle—and no sag results.

When the backcast does not tip downward, no sag results, and the line end is moving the moment the rod begins the forward stroke. This makes it possible to make a good forward cast.

29 CASTING WEIGHTED FLIES AND LEADERS

Trout fishermen often use a leader that may be weighed down with two or more flies, a clump of split shot, and an indicator. This often results in serious tangles. There is a method for throwing this mess for short distances without a tangle.

Make a backcast.

As the line travels back, drop the rod tip down behind you almost to the surface.

Make a smooth sweep of the rod (don't make a normal speed-up-and-stop) on the forward cast. You are going to lob the whole thing, and it is best to direct tip to travel well above your head. Use this technique and you can cast such tackle all day long without a tangle.

30 THE DUMP ROLL CAST

I urge all trout fishermen who want to make longer, drag-free drifts with a nymph or dry fly to perfect this cast. Many consider it to be one of the most effective casts in their arsenal. This cast is especially useful when there is slow holding water along a bank, but there is fast water between you and that quiet water, and you want to drift your fly along that bank.

Bring the rod back in a vertical position, as if you were going to make a normal roll cast. Instead of directing the rod tip to stop well ahead, drive the tip downward in front of you. Imagine you are making a poor roll cast, with the tip stopping in the direction indicated by the arrow.

Note that most of the line has been thrown down in front of you.

The line will roll over, but the entire front end will pile up, creating a lot of slack in the front of the line and leader. This allows a long, drag-free drift of the fly. It takes a little practice to get the fly to land on target and obtain the slack you need. But once you master this cast, I guarantee you'll catch more trout.

31 CASTING INTO THE WIND

Certainly one of the most difficult casts is when you are forced to deliver your fly into a stiff breeze. A large or wide-open loop will make it extremely difficult. To cast effectively in these conditions, the rod should move through a longer stroke, the loop must be as tight as possible, and you need to make a faster haul on the line.

If the cast is directed straight ahead or elevated when throwing into the wind, the leader and line will be blown backward before contacting the water at the end of the cast, when all energy has been expended.

This is one of the rare times when I suggest that you aim the cast directly at the surface where you want the cast to end. This might cause a noisy entry, which will usually be ignored by the fish because the water will be rippled by wind.

The perfect cast into the wind will lay the line and leader straight on to the water. Directing the line downward exposes less of the line to the wind, and prevents the breeze from blowing the line backward and making your cast fall short.

SHORT INDEX